For Arthur, Lucas, and one to come

Text and Images Copyright © by Little Stitches Books

No part of this book may be reproduced in any manner whatsoever without written permission except in the case of brief quotations embodied in critical articles and reviews.

Be the first to hear about new releases and join the Mailing list at LittleStitchesBooks.com

----
ISBN: 978-1-0692837-4-0

First Edition

First, the ingredients!

Welcome, friends! Today, we're making a delicious pot of chicken, rice, and veggie soup. But before we start, let's check our recipe to see what we need!

You'll need:
- 🌿 A drizzle of olive oil
- 🧅 1 onion (sweet)
- 🥕 5-6 thick carrots
- 🌿 1 celery stalk
- 🧄 1 teaspoon of minced garlic (jar minced is okay)
- 🍲 5–8 cups of chicken broth
- 🍗 2 chicken breasts (optional)
- 🍚 1 cup of rice (basmati or brown work great)
- 🥫 1 tin of evaporated milk
- 🌿 A teaspoon each of parsley, thyme, and salt, and a pinch of black pepper

Lets dig up some carrots!

The crew is hard at work, digging up a big, crunchy carrot. Careful team, don't leave any behind!

Carrots start as tiny seeds buried in the soil. When their bright orange tops peek above the ground, it's time to harvest!

<u>Ingredient:</u> 5-6 thick carrots

Garlic Time!

The team is busy gathering fresh garlic from the field! Can you smell that delicious, spicy scent?

Garlic starts as a single clove buried in the dirt. As it grows, tall green leaves stretch toward the sky! When the bottom leaves turn brown, it's time to harvest.

<u>Ingredient:</u> 1 teaspoon of minced garlic

Chopping down Celery!

Timber! Our little lumberjacks have pulled up a tall, crunchy stalk of celery. Now they're working hard to haul it back home!

Celery grows from tiny seeds, or you can regrow it from the bottom of a cut stalk! It stretches up and out of the soil, reaching for the sun.

<u>Ingredient:</u> One whole stalk of celery

Don't Cry, It's Just an Onion!

Deep underground, our tiny miners are hard at work, unearthing a golden onion. Careful, team, this one might make us tear up!

Onions grow beneath the soil, with tall green leaves stretching toward the sun. When chopped, they release a special juice that can make your eyes sting—but don't worry, it's worth it for the flavor!

<u>Ingredient</u>: 1 sweet onion, chopped

Super Spinach Harvest!

Our little farmers are hard at work, using a tiny tractor to gather fresh, leafy spinach for our soup!

Spinach grows in bunches from tiny seeds. Some plants stay small, but others can stretch up to a whole ruler tall!

<u>Ingredient:</u> A couple handfuls of baby spinach

Chilly Chicken!

Brrr! Our tiny workers bundle up as they step into the icy fridge to gather some chicken for our soup!

Chicken breast is a tasty protein that you can buy at the grocery store. It stays fresh in the fridge until it's time to cook!

<u>Ingredient:</u> 2 boneless, skinless chicken breasts (optional)

Magnificent Milk!

Our tiny dairy farmers are hard at work in the barn, checking on the cows and collecting fresh milk!

For this recipe, we need evaporated milk. That means some of the water has been removed, making it extra creamy!

Ingredient: 1 small tin of evaporated milk

Bath Time!

No, not that kind of bath, this one's for our ingredients! Our tiny workers are busy scrubbing the carrots, celery, and spinach to make sure they're squeaky clean.

Since these veggies grow in the dirt, it's always a good idea to give them a rinse in the sink before we cook!

<u>Step:</u> Wash the carrots, celery, and spinach, then set them aside.

More Bath Time?

Guess what? Rice needs a bath too!
It feels like we're giving lots of baths today!

Gently washing rice helps keep the grains from sticking together while cooking. Now that's a clean start!

Step: Gently rinse the rice.

Ingredient: 1 cup (or so) of rice (brown or basmati).

It's Getting Spiced Up!

Our little workers are busy measuring out some dried spices to add a big burst of flavor to the soup!

Spices come from plants, and they're usually dried (or sometimes fresh). Before you measure them, take a sniff! The smell is part of the fun!

<u>Step:</u> Measure the spices and set them aside.

<u>Ingredients:</u> A teaspoon each of parsley, thyme, and salt and a pinch of black pepper (to taste).

Chop Chop!

It's time to peel and chop our nice clean vegetables so they're ready to join the soup!

The onion might have a papery outer layer that needs peeling away.

The carrots can be peeled with a handy peeler, and then it's time to chop!

Step: Peel the onion and carrot. Dice the onion. Chop the carrots and celery into little pieces.

Lets Start Soupin'!

It's time to cook up some soup magic! Let's start heating a pot on the stove.

Once it's nice and hot, add a little oil. Wait just a minute, then toss in the onions and garlic. Stir them around until the onions turn golden and smell so yummy!

Now, it's time to add the rest of the veggies. Stir them all together, and cook for another 3-4 minutes before adding in those tasty spices!

<u>Step:</u> Heat up the oil, fry the onions and garlic, then add the veggies and heat them up. Finally, mix in the spices!

Broth and Boil!

Now that our vegetables and spices are nice and hot, it's time to add in the broth, chicken, and rice!

If the broth doesn't quite cover everything, don't worry, just add a little water or more broth.

Turn up the heat and bring the soup to a boil! Be sure to stir it as you go. After it's boiled for a couple of minutes, turn down the heat a bit to simmer.

<u>Step:</u> Add the broth, rice, and chicken (optional). Bring to a boil, stirring often. Once it's boiled for a couple of minutes, reduce to a simmer, stirring occasionally until the veggies and rice are tender (30 minutes or so).

Finishing Touches!

The soup has been simmering, and now it's time for the final touches!

With an adult, carefully remove the chicken and shred it (it's hot, so be careful!), then, add it back into the pot.

Next, pour in a tin of evaporated milk and give it a good stir. Let it simmer for another minute, and... it's done!

<u>Step:</u> Remove the chicken, shred it, and add it back into the pot with the evaporated milk. Stir it all together.

The Best Part of Making Soup? Sharing!

The soup is ready, and now it's time to share it with friends and family!

Our little workers use a ladle to scoop the soup into bowls. Be careful - it's hot!

Step: Ladle the soup into bowls and serve! It's delicious on its own, or you can enjoy it with some yummy garlic bread.

Yummy Soup!

All the hard work has paid off, and now it's time to enjoy the soup!

Sharing this delicious soup is even more special when you helped make it. Look at those happy faces!

Bon Appétit!

See You Next Time, Friends!

The best part about soup is that you can make it again and again!

Next time, try adding or removing ingredients to make it your own. Or, add some extra cream and blend it into a creamy delight!

The best part about cooking is that you get to choose what goes into your creation!

<u>Bye bye for now!</u>

www.ingramcontent.com/pod-product-compliance
Lightning Source LLC
Chambersburg PA
CBHW041440010526

44118CB00002B/135